More Winnowed Fragments

Simon Pettet

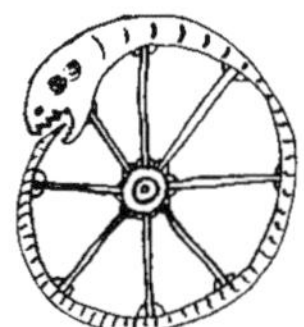

More Winnowed Fragments

Talisman House, Publishers
Jersey City, New Jersey

Published by
Talisman House, Publishers
P.O. Box 3157
Jersey City, New Jersey 07303-3157

Manufactured in the United Sates of America
Printed on acid-free paper

Grateful acknowledgment is made to the editors and publishers of magazines, webzines and broadsides in which many of the poems in this collection first appeared.

CONTENTS

Poem ("Music with cobalt air")

Beau Regard

She

More Winnowed Fragments

My Methodology

I accrue hordes

and then

winnow away,

It is a thankless task,

tho' not without

occult comfort.

There is a cruel, messianic, dim, tribal intransigence

That gains you nothing

There's a bull-headed childish baby-tantrum

That can unleash untold consequences

I am appalled by the darkening of the sky

I watch my love

It is always my love that I watch

I care, I don't bruise you.
I take extraordinary care, but once
In a bus, say, or in the park, or
In a coffee shop, it strikes (me)
The im-poss-ibility
(as you might say)
it could be literally anything, anyplace
an old shoe, a piece of fabric
a woman's face, a man's face

there is some kind of luck tho'
actually impelling us to look
without which our "vaunted intelligence"
might only be secondary
and our "looks"? ha!
our looks?

some of them inflict on them
and some of them pour forth devotion
some are like cats in the yard
regarding bowls of water
we all have to wash

some of them are strict, cruel, insistent,
others, more promising, lackadaisical
some are the tricks
of their fathers and mothers
others not

* * * * * * * * *

and were it not for the pool
we would all be
such smart bunnies
and were it not for the toast
we would all get up each morning
and fix the drips

* * * * * * * * * * *

The real work for the fish is to swim isn't it?
All the rest is "taken care of"
The ship that exists inside a bottle is a
"real" ship

kundalini serpent power in readiness
uncontrollable laughter spasms and crying
wiggy? wired?
pull yourself together man!
The moment so fleeting

Wash your tooth
Wash your rings
Dry your hair
(in the river)
with a raggedy old cloth
Put clean socks on your cold feats (feet)

Sleep in the same bed
with (a mirror) your sister
but never touch (the mirror)

The quest for this gem has as a pre-requisite..

Spotless, keep it spotless

The telepathic schizophrenic
Who suddenly appears
In Doctor Ehrenwald's office

Is not the same as the
Tall thin West African
Who rapped upon your door, dear, Tuesday morning

Discoursing on science-fiction haiku
And promising the secrets
of Pythagorian mathematics

(that was someone else)

Sleep fitful wake grumpy go down stairs cold in dark still morning fill kettle
          tin can
cold water
make tea light fire kindling examine
the early morning light, put on the radio (it is quarter to seven
you are listening to the farming report)

blessèd sleep I know not what you wear or who you are

I imagine you in something extraordinary

slept last night again a baby what do *I* know?
(what is my plot?) all curled up like that
(on a blanket)

Rainstorm
Under-payment
Makes for courtesy on the bus
How does the rabbi save his broad brim hat
From the rain? – Plastic? – ok
I stand no longer secure
Was I ever?

TOMBSTONE

see

I eat

crow

and

stones

wipe

my

tired

eyes

I am

alone..

and you?

The first time that we stayed
In the city we stayed indoors
But I looked out a lot
On an empty lot (and)
Was quiet and kept to myself

We first moved in in the dead of winter
I was like an animal
Needing some place warm
(which of course I never got)

But I do recall golden shafts of light
Upon me
One particular winter's afternoon

Peter Stupid

Orphan Master

Famous For His Tulip

Gardens

Where Now On Broadway

The Equitable Building

Stands

Here we read its signature
on palm leaf manuscripts
peacocks and apes
surrounding us

But if *you* had not come
How would *we* have known?

Firstly, she starts to mutter and twitch
Secondly, her hair falls out (widow's peak,
bald patches). Third, her once-pristine togs
become grimy (regrettably soiled), fourth
she "gives forth foul odours",
Fifth, finally, in rueful old age, she realizes
she can never again capture what she once had
"With that reckless indifference to the world",
she gives up. She curls up under the stars,
she imagines the vast terrible outside void
and her heart's pit-a-pat.

* *

Firstly, he starts to mutter and twitch
Secondly, his hair falls out (widow's peak,
bald patches). Third, his once-pristine togs
become grimy (regrettably soiled), fourth
he "gives forth foul odours"
Fifth, finally, in rueful old age, he realizes
he can never again capture what he once had
"With that reckless indifference to the world".
he gives up. He curls up under the stars,
he imagines the vast terrible outside void
and his heart's pit-a-pat.

Herman,
who had expired
Shortly after midnight
A shudder
What was that?
A ricochet of a heart attack
A flicker of recognition
In the old house
with the books,
on Twenty-Sixth Street

He had lived there so long
He could be forgiven
For being tired

Nobody except his friends
(what few of them)
and himself
had any idea of
who he was!

indeed who he had been

ignorant of the immensity of
all that he'd accomplished

the oceans
but all that was "in another place"
"in another life-time"

funeral Wednesday afternoon at three
internment at Woodlawn Cemetery

Those angels which do not know their father

out of jealousy detain their mother in captivity

confused for centuries, she passes from one female body

into another female body into another female body

JULY ON HORATIO STREET

Last night I spied
the great bard naked
I begged his pardon
For my crass intrusion
I meant to tell him
I loved his work
I'm not a creep
I don't think he heard me
(He didn't *not* hear me)
He was just otherwise engaged
With this complicated process of extinction

* * * * * * * * * * * * *

Last night I spied
the great bard naked
I begged her pardon
For my crass intrusion
I meant to tell her
I loved her work
I'm not a creep
I don't think she heard me
(She didn't *not* hear me)
She was just otherwise engaged
With this complicated process of extinction

the robin and the butterfly

and the leaf and the flame

and the extinction

PASTORAL

It all passes
Ah, but the lasses
These bodies
shall decompose

All's grey
inside and outside
The bird in the bush is
hush,

the mad piper,
silent

as are
The cows in the field .

Is my mother

in the Darby and Joan club

with her final beau

(and some peace at last)?

Is it a winter's chance

(late November)

at the Periphery Dance Hall?

La luce terra cotta olive green
Fig tree quiet Tuscan morning birdsong
Church bell toll butterfly zig-zag
(cars on the road zoom by and then returning to silence)
paving stones, dappled shadows

POEM ("send the endorphins to the foot please")

send the endorphins to the foot please
that's where the pain is

negotiating, I stumbled
and fear I may have bruised something

tho' what *is* the Latin name for
that mysterious connective tissue

bless you – that we all possess?

POEM ("Fortunate proximity of lives..")

Fortunate proximity of lives
Lived in quiet adoration
At rest, jump up on my pillow here, quick,
This spot is your spot, dear, this
Book that I wasn't really reading.
Unforgettable, rare and mysterious (as purring is)
So, this is the lesson that you came to teach

DUNS SCOTIUS ON THE FULL MOON

The eye that lights up the sky is wide open tonight. I think,
I blink
and the rhythmic breathing in the dark of the old guy
in the corner is muted now.

Perhaps he is a dog? Perhaps not.
Shall we find out? We examine his ears
We examine our own ears. We listen tight
to the sounds of a circulating digestion

Since the moon is, we all know, a form of cheese
but what *kind* of cheese?
and there are olives on our plate (the mauve ones)
and we have drunk moon water and supped
Are we crackers to attest so?

The books on the sidewalk are dutifully arranged.

The officer is a moonlighter because he works at the other precinct.

Dance performers from around the world are advertised on a torn poster. I can't see them though since my dog is blind. I make a wish. I wish for another one. The tethered akita is granted a reprieve. All of this all the time. Every conceivable moment. All the worlds you'd ever want to know

mention to the girl in the vets
about the butterflies
and she's excited!

wants to,
but has never done it before
but is willing to try (tho)

Freed from the drive-in prison of single-mindedness
He turns effortlessly to the highway drama
Of the heart's debate with the so-called "verifiable" world...

A FIT OF PIQUE

Carefully printed cards are made up
Embossed with the visitors' names.
Elaborate procedures for stalling
are then devised. Regrets are sent.
But will it all stand up under vigorous
cross-examination?

She stopped talking (to him) because he stopped listening.
He stopped listening because she got sober and wiser.
It's a mug's game (a mug's game?). It's a shame.
Those letters were perfect
and now no one's going to own them.

If

I had obeyed the sun

I would've been permitted to shed my skin

without such trials (no sweat!)

and to have (naturally) stayed smooth forever

But,

since I have supped on sugar and aniseed,

and licorice and sherbert,

I am forbidden to stand naked in consequence.

Two and a half fish

Leaping out of the river

A
Scension

Life rises

To a certain pitch

"My soul, what's lighter than a feather? Wind
Than wind? The fire. And what than fire? The mind
What's lighter than the mind? A thought. Than thought?
This bubble world. What than this bubble? Naught."
(Francis Quarles – epigram to A Pair of Balances)

If we had our copper vessel perfectly round

And well closed

We should have fixed Mercury with the Moon

– but we didn't!

* *

"Approximately 75 per cent

of the waking consciousness

is consumed

with the monitoring

of physical functions"

"either wanting it

or already in possession of it

– or, rather, both"

* *

It is when the extreme point of restlessness

is reached

that grace comes

at a terrific speed.

The creative magic of the body
Is a thing of wonder
Says my friend Fran
Thinking of Brancusi

I don't yet know what
Form it'll take
But when I *do* know!

The ripest of the blackberries
Both delights the child and seduces and appalls
(he is quite ignorant of course
and quite surprised by those adoring
adjacent stinging nettles

"The just hand
Is a precious ointment
And the evidence of scars
Is not *itself* proof.."

Who wrote that book
(about staying alive
In the body)

You did

Music with cobalt air

Let *her* sit there

Beside the rocks,

Painting her pots

I love her

Because she

gives me

Permission

And she excites –

We excite

In each other..Ah!

Curiosity!

BEAU REGARD

Her skinny body is white as a harvest moon,
Clear as a crystal goblet, radiating light
She has one face, two hands with slender fingers,
bright eyes, she looks at me,
she's not afraid to look at me
nor I to look back

SHE

She
is the very picture of fortitude
and on her head wears one of several
floppy hats,
drapes her form in glorious scarlet
and is at ease,
when bending down and calmly placing
either one or both her hands
upon the stormy animal's mouth